W9-AHF-965

Political Wit

POLITICAL WIT

Text compiled by Steven Gauge.

Illustrations by Ian Baker.

Summersdale Publishers Ltd
46 West Street
Chichester
West Sussex
PO19 1RP
UK

www.summersdale.com

Printed and bound by CPI Group (UK) Ltd, Croydon, CR0 4YY

ISBN: 978-1-84953-188-7

Political Wit

Quips and Quotes from the Back Benches and Beyond

Steven Gauge

Illustrations by Ian Baker

summersdale

Contents

Editor's Note

As the old joke goes, you can always tell when politicians are lying by watching to see if they open their mouths. Luckily for us, it seems that our political leaders are just as good at raising a laugh as they are at raising our taxes. Whether wrestling with the great affairs of state or honing memorable sound bites for the modern media machine, the political class can produce some great gags and the occasional gaffe to make us all chuckle whatever side of the fence we are on.

So, whether you are red, blue, orange, green or somewhere in between, the choice is yours: who will get your vote in the ballot for the brightest and best of the political wits?

THE ART OF POLITICS

A politician is
a person who
approaches every
subject with an
open mouth.

Adlai Stevenson

A lot has been said about politics; some of it complimentary, but most of it accurate.

Eric Idle

The art of politics consists in knowing precisely when it is necessary to hit an opponent slightly below the belt.

Konrad Adenauer

Politics is not the art of the possible. It consists in choosing between the disastrous and the unpalatable.

John Kenneth Galbraith

Politics is supposed
to be the second-
oldest profession.
I have come to realise
that it bears a very
close resemblance
to the first.

Ronald Reagan

MP

In politics, guts is all.

Barbara Castle

The challenge is to practise politics as the art of making what appears to be impossible, possible.

Hillary Clinton

Get the advice of everybody whose advice is worth having – they are very few – and then do what you think best yourself.

Charles Stewart Parnell

Politics is the art of preventing people from taking part in affairs which properly concern them.

Paul Valéry

Politics is the art of looking for trouble, finding it everywhere, diagnosing it wrongly and applying unsuitable remedies.

Ernest Benn

When a politician is in Opposition he is an expert on the means to some end; and when he is in office he is an expert on the obstacles to it.

Gilbert K. Chesterton

Always be sincere, even
if you don't mean it.

Harry S. Truman

'Politics' is made up of two words;
'poli', which is Greek for 'many', and
'tics', which are bloodsucking insects.

Gore Vidal

The game of politics is to make
you afraid so that you don't think.

Michelle Obama

Politics is the gentle art of getting votes from the poor and campaign funds from the rich, by promising to protect each from the other.

Oscar Ameringer

Politicians are people who, when they see light at the end of the tunnel, go out and buy some more tunnel.

John Quinton

Democracy means government by discussion, but it is only effective if you can stop people talking.

Clement Attlee

NICE WORK IF YOU CAN GET IT

Being an MP is the sort of job all working-class parents want for the children – clean, indoors and no heavy lifting.

Diane Abbott

Politician is perhaps the only profession for which no preparation is thought necessary.

Robert Louis Stevenson

It's a pity, as my husband says, that more politicians are not bastards by birth instead of vocation.

Katherine Whitehorn

He knows nothing; and he thinks he knows everything. That points clearly to a political career.

George Bernard Shaw

Being in politics is like being a football coach: you have to be smart enough to understand the game, and dumb enough to think it's important.

Eugene McCarthy

To succeed pre-eminently in English public life it is necessary to conform to either the popular image of a bookie or of a clergyman.

Malcolm Muggeridge

In the last parliament, the House of Commons had more MPs called John than all the women MPs put together.

Tessa Jowell

Under every stone
lurks a politician.

Aristophanes

A politician is a man who understands government, and it takes a politician to run a government. A statesman is a politician who's been dead ten to fifteen years.

Harry S. Truman

A politician is a fellow who will lay down your life for his country.

Texas Guinan

Vote for the man who promises least;
he'll be the least disappointing.

Bernard Baruch

Suppose you were an idiot. And
suppose you were a member of
Congress. But I repeat myself.

Mark Twain

My grandfather once told me that there were two kinds of people: those who do the work and those who take the credit. He told me to try to be in the first group; there was much less competition.

Indira Ghandi

FOR THE SAKE OF ARGUMENT

A good cause has to be careful of the company it keeps.

Rebecca West

In politics stupidity is not a handicap.

Napoleon Bonaparte

Whenever you find that you are
on the side of the majority, it
is time to pause and reflect.

Mark Twain

Sanity is not statistical. Being in a minority, even a minority of one, did not make you mad.

Winston Smith, in George Orwell's *1984*

If everybody is thinking alike, then somebody isn't thinking.

General George S. Patton

The test of a first-rate intelligence is the ability to hold two opposed ideas in mind at the same time and still retain the ability to function.

F. Scott Fitzgerald

TAX CUTS
TAX RISES

I myself have never been able to find out precisely what feminism is: I only know that people call me a feminist whenever I express sentiments that differentiate me from a doormat or a prostitute.

Rebecca West

Your voices are not worth a rat's squeak, either in Parliament or out of it, till you have some ideas to utter with them.

John Ruskin

I saw David Owen on television the other week. He was heckling a small number of bystanders in Torquay. And then I realised they weren't bystanders – they were his own party.

Kenneth Baker

I am extraordinarily patient, provided I get my own way in the end.

Margaret Thatcher

What I want is men who will support me when I am in the wrong.

Lord Melbourne to a fellow politician who had said, 'I will support you as long as you are in the right.'

I cannot help it if every time the Opposition are asked to name their weapons they pick boomerangs.

Iain MacLeod

Assassination is the extreme form of political censorship.

George Bernard Shaw

VERY CIVIL SERVANTS

Here lies a civil
servant. He was civil
To everyone, and
servant to the devil.

C. H. Sisson

The business of the Civil Service is the orderly management of decline.

William Armstrong

The Civil Service is a bit like a rusty weathercock. It moves with opinion and then stays where it is until another wind moves it in a different direction.

Tony Benn

You've just given me twenty reasons why I can't do this; I'm sure that clever chaps like you can go away and produce twenty good reasons why I can.

Ernest Bevin to his civil servants

Guidelines for bureaucrats:
(1) When in charge, ponder.
(2) When in trouble, delegate.
(3) When in doubt, mumble.

James H. Boren

Britain has invented a new missile. It's called the civil servant. It doesn't work and it can't be fired.

General Sir Walter Walker

Give a civil servant a good case and he'll wreck it with clichés, bad punctuation, double negatives and convoluted apology.

Alan Clark

The ideal civil servant should always be colourless, odourless and tasteless.

Roger Peyrefitte

You must think the unthinkable,
but always wear a dark suit
when presenting the results.

Dick Ross

Politicians often believe that their
world is the real one. Officials
sometimes take a different view.

Lord Rothschild

Dennis Skinner: How many civil
servants are a) men and b) women?
Tim Renton: All of them.

In answer to a parliamentary question

UP CLOSE AND PERSONAL

Bring us three Buck's Fizzes and keep the change.

Alan Clark to Sir Geoffrey Howe, dressed in a dinner jacket

The House has noticed the Prime Minister's remarkable transformation in the past few weeks – from Stalin to Mr Bean.

Vince Cable on Gordon Brown at Prime Minister's Question Time

Dennis Skinner: What I want to know, Mr Speaker, is why you allow this 'ere pompous git... [referring to David Owen]
Mr Speaker: That, sir, is unparliamentary language. I demand you withdraw it.
Dennis Skinner: In deference to you, Mr Speaker, I withdraw 'pompous'.

Far better to keep your mouth shut and let everyone think you're stupid than to open it and leave no doubt.

Norman Tebbit on Dennis Skinner

A pudgy puffball.

Alan Clark on Kenneth Clarke

Might as well have a corncob up his arse.

Alan Clark on Douglas Hurd

The trouble with Michael is that he had to buy his own furniture.

Michael Jopling on Michael Heseltine, quoted by Alan Clark in his diaries and often misattributed to him

... like being savaged by a dead sheep.

Denis Healey on being attacked by Geoffrey Howe

He's passed from rising hope to elder statesman without any intervening period whatsoever.

Michael Foot on David Steel

The ego has landed.

Frank Dobson on Ken Livingstone

Peter Mandelson is someone who can skulk in broad daylight.

Simon Hoggart

She is clearly the best man among them.

Barbara Castle on Margaret Thatcher and her rivals for the leadership of the Conservative Party

Not even her best friends would describe her as a glamour puss, whose face would be likely to turn on many voters. Except perhaps those who are members of the British Horse Society.

John Junor on Margaret Beckett

Unless the country sees evidence soon of his willingness to stand firm, he will go down in history as Mr Pussy Foot.

Cyril Smith on Michael Foot

A man who boasts that he won the Most Boring Politician of the Year award from *Trucker's Weekly* magazine, two years in a row.

Ann Treneman on Alistair Darling

He is like a hollow Easter egg with no bag of sweets inside... He's nothing. He's no one.

Charlie Brooker on David Cameron

At the moment the Labour leader
has two major problems to overcome.
How he looks and what he says.

Peter Bingle on Ed Miliband

I've met serial killers and professional
assassins and nobody scared
me as much as Mrs T.

Ken Livingstone on Margaret Thatcher

A big cat detained briefly in
a poodle parlour, sharpening
her claws on the velvet.

Matthew Parris on Lady Thatcher

John Major is to leadership what Cyril Smith is to hang-gliding.

John Prescott

He delivers all his statements as though auditioning for the speaking clock.

Stephen Glover on John Major

When I hear the name of
Richard Body I hear the sound
of flapping white coats.

John Major

I wouldn't vote for Ken
Livingstone if he were running
for mayor of Toytown.

Arthur Scargill

John Major, Norman Lamont:
I wouldn't spit in their mouths
if their teeth were on fire.

Rodney Bickerstaffe

'Life is better under the Tories'
sounds to me like one of Steve
Norris's chat-up lines.

John Prescott

I suspect language isn't
his first language.

Linda Smith on John Prescott

The trouble with you, John, is that your spine does not reach your brain.

Margaret Thatcher to Conservative backbencher John Whittingdale

He asked, 'Do you ever come down to London? If you ever come down you must come to Number 10 and meet me and Sarah... ' Well, I just looked at him. I didn't like to say it, but all I could think was, 'I don't think you'll be there.'

Gillian ('Bigotgate') Duffy on Gordon Brown, speaking to the *Daily Mail*

The weak are a long time in politics.

Neil Shand on John Gummer

I asked the simple question whether it was really Mr Tebbit's desire always to give his imitation of a semi-house-trained polecat.

Michael Foot on Norman Tebbit

Mrs Currie loses an enormous number of opportunities to remain silent.

Gerald Kaufman on Edwina Currie

... like putting Dracula in charge of a blood transfusion service.

Eric Varley on Norman Tebbit's move to the Department of Employment

EVERY UNDERDOG HAS ITS DAY

No one can make you feel inferior without your consent.

Eleanor Roosevelt

If anyone believes that our smiles involve abandonment of the teaching of Marx, Engels and Lenin, he deceives himself. Those who wait for that must wait until a shrimp learns to whistle.

Nikita Khrushchev

That would be a good idea.

Mahatma Gandhi, when asked what he thought of modern civilisation

When I give food to the poor
they call me a saint. When I
ask why the poor have no food
they call me a communist.

Hélder Câmara

History teaches us that men and
nations behave wisely once they
have exhausted all the alternatives.

Abba Eban

We are not asking for superiority
for we have always had that;
all we ask is equality.

Nancy Astor

It is better to die on your feet than to live on your knees.

Dolores Ibárruri ('La Pasionaria')

You should never have your best trousers on when you go out to fight for freedom and truth.

Henrik Ibsen

Anarchism is a game at which the police can beat you.

George Bernard Shaw

In this world, I'd rather live
two days like a tiger than two
hundred years like a sheep.

Tipu Sultan, sixteenth-century southern Indian ruler

Most of us women like men, you
know; it's just that we find them
a constant disappointment.

Clare Short

ALL WAR IS DECEPTION

Let him who
desires peace,
prepare for war.

Vegetius, fourth-century Roman military expert

Anyone who isn't confused doesn't really understand the situation.

Ed Murrow on the Vietnam problem

Wars are popular. Contractors make profits; the aristocracy gleans honour.

Ramsay MacDonald

A nation is only at peace when it is at war.

Hugh Kingsmill

Sixty years ago this week Hitler invaded Poland. This led to the creation of *The History Channel*.

Jay Leno

What difference does it make to the dead, the orphans and the homeless, whether the mad destruction is wrought under the name of totalitarianism or the holy name of liberty or democracy?

Mahatma Gandhi

They couldn't hit an elephant at this dist...

Last words of Union commander General John Sedgwick, spoken as he was watching enemy troops at the Battle of Spotsylvania Court House

The whole history of the world is summed up in the fact that, when nations are strong, they are not always just, and when they wish to be just, they are no longer strong.

Winston Churchill

I can't believe that war is the best solution. No one won the last war and no one will win the next war.

Eleanor Roosevelt

They found more dangerous chemicals in Coca-Cola's Dasani mineral water than they did in the whole of Iraq.

Robin Cook

LOOK-MORE WEAPONS OF THIRST DESTRUCTION!

The quickest way of ending
a war is to lose it.

George Orwell

War is a very rough game, but
I think that politics is worse.

Lord Montgomery

Bloody well get on and do it,
otherwise I'll headbutt you!

Mo Mowlam, overheard speaking to Sinn Fein's Gerry
Adams during the 'Good Friday' peace negotiations

I'm not worried about the
Third World War. That's the
Third World's problem.

Jimmy Carr

Presentationally, Bill Clinton is
a US president to die for. The
truth is, far too many have.

Jon Snow

I've spent my life fighting the Germans and fighting the politicians. It is much easier to fight the Germans.

Field Marshal Montgomery

The Admiralty has demanded six, the Treasury said we could only have four so we compromised on eight.

Winston Churchill on the finer points of defence procurement

One to mislead the public, another to mislead the Cabinet and the third to mislead itself.

H. H. Asquith on discovering that the War Office kept three separate sets of figures

THE GLOVES ARE OFF

A greater love hath no man than this, that he lay down his friends for his life.

Jeremy Thorpe on Harold Macmillan's sacking of seven members of the Cabinet in the so-called 'Night of the Long Knives'

Shot any dogs lately?

Cyril Smith to Jeremy Thorpe, the Liberal Party leader forced to resign following accusations of involvement in a plot to murder his alleged lover Norman Scott, which resulted in the death of a Great Dane called Rinka

Baldwin often times stumbles over the truth, but he always picks himself up and hurries on as if nothing had happened.

Winston Churchill

Did you ever hear of a man who having got rid of a boil on the back of his neck ever wants it back again?

Lord Salisbury on the possibility of re-employing Randolph Churchill

Winston has devoted the best years of his life to preparing his impromptu speeches.

F. E. Smith on Winston Churchill

He can't see
a belt without
hitting below it.

Margot Asquith on Lloyd George

He aroused every feeling
except trust.

A. J. P. Taylor on Lloyd George

This high official, all allow,
Is grossly overpaid;
There wasn't any Board, and now
There isn't any Trade.

A. P. Herbert on the President of the Board of Trade

This extraordinary figure of our time, this syren, this goat-footed bard, this half-human visitor to our age from the hag-ridden magic and enchanted woods of Celtic antiquity.

John Maynard Keynes on Lloyd George

Like a village fiddler after Paganini.

Harold Nicolson on Attlee compared to Churchill

He was not only a bore; he bored for England.

Malcolm Muggeridge on Anthony Eden

A modest man who has much
to be modest about.

Winston Churchill on Clement Attlee

An empty taxi arrived at 10
Downing Street, and when the
door was opened, Attlee got out.

Attributed to Winston Churchill
although strongly denied by him

Nancy Astor: If I were your wife I
would put poison in your coffee.
Winston Churchill: And if I were
your husband I would drink it.

For twenty years he has held a season ticket on the line of least resistance and has gone wherever the train of events has carried him, lucidly justifying himself at whatever point he happened to find himself.

Leo Amery on Herbert Henry Asquith

Harold Wilson is going around the country stirring up apathy.

William Whitelaw

... unfortunately whenever he was getting warm, the Irish secretly changed the Question.

W. C. Sellar and R. J. Yeatman (*1066 and All That*), on Gladstone and the Irish Question

He speaks to me as if I was a public meeting.

Queen Victoria on Gladstone

The difference between a misfortune and a calamity is this: if Gladstone fell into the Thames, it would be a misfortune. But if someone dragged him out again, that would be a calamity.

Benjamin Disraeli on William Gladstone

If I saw Mr Haughey buried at midnight at a crossroads with a stake driven through his heart – politically speaking – I should continue to wear a clove of garlic round my neck, just in case.

Conor Cruise O'Brien speaking to *The Observer*

Don't be so humble.
You're not that great.

Golda Meir to Moshe Dayan

He has the gift of compressing the largest amount of words into the smallest amount of thought.

Winston Churchill on Ramsay MacDonald

When they circumcised Herbert Samuel they threw away the wrong bit.

David Lloyd George

If it's a boy I'll call him John. If it's a girl I'll call her Mary. But if, as I suspect, it's only a bag of wind, I'll call it F. E. Smith.

Lord Chief Justice Stewart to F. E. Smith after he commented on the size of Stewart's stomach and asked 'What's it to be, a boy or girl?'

MY COUNTRY, RIGHT OR WRONG

The great nations have always acted like gangsters, and the small nations like prostitutes.

Stanley Kubrick

One of the myths of the British Parliament is that there are three parties there. I can assure you from bitter personal experience there are six hundred and twenty-nine.

Horace Maybray King

Welcome to Britain's new political order. No passion... No right. No left. Just multi-hued blancmange.

Austin Mitchell

In England all is permitted that
is not expressly prohibited...
in Germany all is prohibited
unless expressly permitted and
in France all is permitted that
is expressly prohibited.

Robert Megarry

Illegal aliens have always
been a problem in the United
States. Ask any Indian.

Robert Orben

A good nationalist should look upon the slugs in the garden much the same way as she looks on the English in Ireland.

Constance Markievicz, known as the Countess of Irish Freedom

I want the whole of Europe to have one currency; it will make trading much easier.

Napoleon I

This island is made mainly of coal and surrounded by fish. Only an organizing genius could produce a shortage of coal and fish at the same time.

Aneurin Bevan

Nobody ever celebrated Devolution Day.

Alex Salmond on his dream of Scottish independence

England's not a bad country… It's just a mean, cold, ugly, divided, tired, clapped out, post-imperial, post-industrial slag heap.

Margaret Drabble

America is a large, friendly dog in a very small room. Every time it wags its tail it knocks over a chair.

Arnold Toynbee

Living next to you is in some ways like sleeping with an elephant. No matter how friendly and even-tempered the beast, one is affected by every twitch and grunt.

Pierre Trudeau on the relationship between his country, Canada, and the USA

Let me tell you something that we Israelis have against Moses. He took us forty years through the desert in order to bring us to the one spot in the Middle East that has no oil!

Golda Meir

Kenneth Clarke: Isn't it terrible about losing to the Germans at our national sport, Prime Minister?
Margaret Thatcher: I shouldn't worry too much – we've beaten them twice this century at theirs.

What a pity, when Christopher Columbus discovered America, that he ever mentioned it.

Margot Asquith

Americans have different ways of saying things. They say 'elevator', we say 'lift'... they say 'president', we say 'stupid psychopathic git'.

Alexei Sayle

Put three Zionists in a room and they will form four political parties.

Levi Eshkol

THE UNITED SLIGHTS OF AMERICA

Poor George, he can't help it – he was born with a silver foot in his mouth.

Ann Richards on George Bush

There they are. See no evil,
hear no evil, and... evil.

Bob Dole on seeing former Presidents
Carter, Ford and Nixon

If you think Daddy had
trouble with 'the vision thing',
wait till you meet this one.

Molly Ivins and Lou Dubose on George W. Bush

Nixon's motto was: If two wrongs don't make a right, try three.

Norman Cousins

Gerry Ford is so dumb that he can't fart and chew gum at the same time.

Lyndon B. Johnson

He slept more than any other president, whether by day or by night. Nero fiddled, but Coolidge only snored.

H. L. Mencken on Calvin Coolidge

He'll double-cross that bridge when he comes to it.

Oscar Levant

If there had been any formidable body of cannibals in the country he would have promised to provide them with free missionaries fattened at the taxpayer's expense.

H. L. Mencken on Harry S. Truman

WE'RE GOING TO NEED A BIGGER POT!

The kind of politician who would cut down a redwood tree and then mount the stump and make a speech on conservation.

Adlai Stevenson on Richard Nixon

Donald Trump often talks about running as a Republican, which is surprising; I just assumed he was running as a joke.

Seth Meyers

I think it's about time we voted for senators with breasts. After all, we've been voting for boobs long enough.

Clarie Sargent, Arizona senatorial candidate

Clinton lied. A man might forget where he parks or where he lives, but he never forgets oral sex, no matter how bad it is.

Barbara Bush

Blair is like a hotel greeter. Clinton did the same thing to perfection, while stroking the bottom of the nearest secretary.

J. G. Ballard

Richard Nixon is a no-good, lying bastard. He can lie out of both sides of his mouth at the same time, and if he ever caught himself telling the truth, he'd lie just to keep his hand in.

Harry S. Truman

IT'S THE ECONOMY, STUPID

Politics is the art
of turning influence
into affluence.

Philander Chase Johnson

You and I come by road or rail, but economists travel on infrastructure.

Margaret Thatcher

Over eighty-five per cent of all statistics are made up on the spot.

David Mitchell

Recession is when you have to tighten the belt. Depression is when there is no belt to tighten. We are probably in the next degree of collapse when there are no trousers as such.

Boris Pankin on Russia in 1992

Some of the jam we thought was for tomorrow, we've already eaten.

Tony Benn

Government is like a baby. An alimentary canal with a big appetite at one end and no sense of responsibility at the other.

Ronald Reagan

Blessed are the young, for they will inherit the national debt.

President Herbert Hoover

Bachelors should be heavily taxed. It's not fair that some men should be happier than others.

Oscar Wilde

The rich require an abundant supply of the poor.

Voltaire

To those who have found breakfast with difficulty and do not know where to find dinner, intricate questions of politics are a matter of comparatively secondary interest.

Lord Salisbury

But this 'long run' is a misleading guide to current affairs. 'In the long run' we are all dead.

John Maynard Keynes

Unfortunately monetarism, like Marxism, suffered the only fate that for a theory is worse than death: it was put into practice.

Ian Gilmour

A government that robs Peter to pay Paul can always depend on the support of Paul.

George Bernard Shaw

Trickle-down theory – the less than elegant metaphor that if one feeds the horse enough oats, some will pass through to the road for the sparrows.

John Kenneth Galbraith

There are two dead bodies on a motorway. One cat and one banker. There was very little difference between the corpses, except for skid marks around the cat.

Vince Cable

If all economists were laid end to end, they would not reach a conclusion.

George Bernard Shaw

There is no art which
one government
sooner learns of
another than that
of draining money
from the pockets
of the people.

Adam Smith

SWAG

It's a recession when your neighbour loses his job; it's a depression when you lose yours.

Harry S. Truman

Everybody is always in favour of general economy and particular expenditure.

Anthony Eden

Making a speech on economics is a bit like pissing down your leg. It seems hot to you but never to anyone else.

Lyndon B. Johnson

TRUE BLUE

Conservatives are not necessarily stupid, but most stupid people are Conservatives.

John Stuart Mill

A Conservative is a man with two perfectly good legs who, however, has never learned to walk forward.

Franklin D. Roosevelt

Conservative n. A statesman who is enamoured of existing evils, as distinguished from the Liberal, who wishes to replace them with others.

Ambrose Bierce

The only thing that was growing then were the lines of coke in front of boy George and the rest of the Tories.

Dennis Skinner on the economic record of the Conservatives in the 1980s

If capitalism depended on
the intellectual quality of the
Conservative party, it would end
about lunchtime tomorrow.

Tony Benn

My epitaph must be: 'Died of writing
inane letters to empty-headed
Conservative Associations'. It is a
miserable death to look forward to.

Lord Salisbury

A Conservative is a man who
believes that nothing should
be done for the first time.

Alfred E. Wiggam

A Conservative is a man who sits and thinks, mostly sits.

Woodrow Wilson

Most Tories seem to think that 'ethics' is a county near Middlesex.

John Prescott

They are nothing else but a load of kippers – two-faced, with no guts.

Eric Heffer on the Conservatives

The only black guy I ever saw in Conservative Central Office was the doorman – now even he has gone.

John Taylor

WE'LL KEEP THE RED FLAG FLYING HERE

The typical Socialist
is... a prim little
man with a white-
collar job, usually a
secret teetotaller
and often with
vegetarian leanings...

George Orwell

The only leaders Labour loves are dead ones.

Robert Harris

The longest suicide note in history.

Gerald Kaufman on Labour's 1983 manifesto

Socialism is nothing but the capitalism of the lower classes.

Oswald Spengler

I too have tried to be a Marxist but common sense kept breaking in.

A. J. P. Taylor

Socialism can only arrive by bicycle.

José Antonio Viera-Gallo

For Socialists, going to bed with the Liberals is like having oral sex with a shark.

Larry Zolf

Voting for New Labour is like helping an old lady across the road while screaming 'Get a move on!'

Boy George

Blair goes one way, Brown goes the other way and bang goes the third way.

Michael Howard

The function of socialism is to raise suffering to a higher level.

Norman Mailer

BEARDS AND SANDALS

As usual the Liberals offer a mixture of sound and original ideas. Unfortunately none of the sound ideas is original and none of the original ideas is sound.

Harold Macmillan

Attacking the Liberals is a difficult business, involving all the hazards of wrestling with a greased pig at a village fair, and then insulting the vicar.

Chris Patten

We know what happens to people who stay in the middle of the road. They get run down.

Aneurin Bevan

Liberalism is trust of the
people tempered by prudence.
Conservatism is distrust of the
people tempered by fear.

William E. Gladstone

If the fence is strong
enough I'll sit on it.

Cyril Smith

If God had been
a Liberal, there
wouldn't have been
Ten Commandments;
there would have been
Ten Suggestions.

Malcolm Bradbury and Christopher Bigsby

SUGGESTION
BOX

In the Members' Dining Room,
the Conservatives eat at one end,
the Labour Party at the other,
while the Liberals wait at table.

Gyles Brandreth

Interviewer (in 2008): 'What's
your favourite joke?'
David Cameron: 'Nick Clegg.'

PLAGUE ON BOTH YOUR HOUSES

Politicians are the same all over. They promise to build a bridge where there is no river.

Nikita Khrushchev

If they will stop telling lies about the Democrats, we will stop telling the truth about them.

Adlai Stevenson on the US Republicans

Any party which takes credit for the rain must not be surprised if its opponents blame it for the drought.

Dwight D. Morrow

A man who has both feet planted firmly in the air can be safely called a Liberal as opposed to the Conservative, who has both feet firmly planted in his mouth.

Jacques Barzun

If a Conservative is a Liberal who's been mugged, a Liberal is a Conservative who's been arrested.

Tom Wolfe

Under capitalism, man exploits man. Under communism, it's just the opposite.

John Kenneth Galbraith

There are far too many men in politics and not enough elsewhere.

Hermione Gingold

When in that House M. P.'s divide,
If they've a brain and cerebellum, too,
They've got to leave
that brain outside,
And vote just as their
leaders tell 'em to.
But then the prospect of a lot
Of dull M. P.'s in close proximity,
All thinking for themselves, is what
No man can face with equanimity.
Then let's rejoice with loud
Fal la – Fal la la!
That Nature always does contrive –
Fal lal la!
That every boy and every gal
That's born into the world alive
Is either a little Liberal
Or else a little Conservative!
Fal lal la!

Private Willis' song from *Iolanthe*
by Gilbert and Sullivan

Democracy's the worst form of government, except for all the others.

Winston Churchill

We hang the petty thieves and appoint the great ones to public office.

Aesop

You're standing on top of a cliff with a Liberal Democrat and a Tory. Which one do you push off first? Answer: the Tory. It's always business before pleasure.

Martin Salter

The reason there are so few female politicians is that it is too much trouble to put make-up on two faces.

Maureen Murphy

HEY! WATCH WHAT YOU'RE DOING!!

The louder he talked of his honour, the faster we counted our spoons.

Ralph Waldo Emerson on the typical politician

What's the difference between a supermarket trolley and a politician? You can get more food and drink into a politician.

Steve Pound

There's an old saying that if all the politicians in the world were laid end to end, they'd still be lying.

Fred Allen

SOMEONE TO WATCH OVER ME

Democracy is the theory that the common people know what they want, and they deserve to get it good and hard.

H. L. Mencken

When great men get drunk
with a theory, it is the little men
who have the headache.

Lord Salisbury

Giving money and power to
government is like giving whisky
and car keys to teenage boys.

P. J. O'Rourke

The nine most terrifying words in the
English language are 'I'm from the
government and I'm here to help'.

Ronald Reagan

I believe there is something
out there watching over us.
Unfortunately, it's the government.

Woody Allen

The only good government... is
a bad one in a hell of a fright.

Joyce Cary

Power tends to corrupt, and
absolute power corrupts
absolutely. Great men are
almost always bad men.

Lord Acton

There is nowhere
in the world where
sleep is so deep as
in the libraries of the
House of Commons.

Henry 'Chips' Channon

SHHHHHHH!..
ZZZZZZZZZZZZZZ

An election is coming. Universal peace is declared and the foxes have a sincere interest in prolonging the lives of the poultry.

George Eliot

Democracy means simply the bludgeoning of the people by the people for the people.

Oscar Wilde

THE DARK ARTS

Get your facts first, and then you can distort them as much as you please.

Mark Twain

We know that Prime Ministers
are wedded to the truth but
like other married couples
they sometimes live apart.

Saki

I thought you were the original
professor of rotational medicine.

Rhodri Morgan to Bernard Ingham

The result of recent experience
is that if you wish to keep a secret
you must say nothing 1. To
Cabinet Ministers 2. To Foreign
Diplomats 3. To the War Office.

Lord Salisbury

A false report, if believed during three days, may be of great service to a government.

Catherine de' Medici

All I say is, if you cannot ride two horses you have no right in the circus.

James Maxton

The illegal we do immediately. The unconstitutional takes a little longer.

Henry Kissinger

There are three kinds of lies:
lies, damned lies and statistics.

Benjamin Disraeli

Our old friend economical...
with the *actualité*.

Alan Clark

We should put the spin doctors in spin clinics, where they can meet other spin patients and be treated by spin consultants. The rest of us can get on with the proper democratic process.

Tony Benn

When a man says he approves of something in principle, it means he hasn't the slightest intention of putting it into practice.

Otto von Bismarck

When I want a peerage, I shall buy it like an honest man.

Lord Northcliffe

You can fool some of the people all of the time, and those are the ones you want to concentrate on.

George W. Bush

Alastair Campbell was a brilliant press officer, a master of media manipulation, and was even kind enough to write this quote for me.

John O'Farrell

Alastair Campbell's memoirs could be worth a lot of money. Not only does he know where the bodies are buried, he buried many of them.

Iain Dale

BLOODY VOTERS

Vote early.
Vote often.

John Van Buren

The trouble with the world is that the stupid are cocksure and the intelligent are full of doubt.

Bertrand Russell

Every government is a parliament of whores. The trouble is, in a democracy the whores are us.

P. J. O'Rourke

No one in this world, so far as I know... has ever lost money by underestimating the intelligence of the great masses of the plain people.

H. L. Mencken

You can fool too many of the people too much of the time.

James Thurber

Toute nation a le gouvernement qu'elle mérite.
Every country has the government it deserves.

Joseph de Maistre

I find most of them boring, petty, malign, clumsily conspiratorial and parochial to a degree that cannot be surpassed in any part of the United Kingdom.

Alan Clark on Tory constituency associations

I did not enter the Labour Party forty-seven years ago to have our manifesto written by Dr Mori, Dr Gallup and Mr Harris.

Tony Benn

About one fifth of the people are against everything all the time.

Robert F. Kennedy

There's a lot of bleeding idiots in t'country and they deserve some representation.

Bill Stones

Hell, I never vote for anybody,
I always vote against.

W. C. Fields

In democracy everyone has the right to be represented, even the jerks.

Chris Patten

If my critics saw me walking over the Thames they would say it was because I couldn't swim.

Margaret Thatcher

Too bad all the
people who know how
to run the country
are busy driving cabs
and cutting hair.

George Burns

FLOATING VOTERS?...
I HAD ONE OF THEM
IN THE BACK OF MY
CAB....
TAXI

Some people eat eggs, I wear them.

John Major, after an egg made a mess of
his suit during an election campaign

The only thing I like about
rich people is their money.

Nancy Astor

Democracy substitutes election
by the incompetent many for
appointment by the corrupt few.

George Bernard Shaw

DID I SAY THAT OUT LOUD?

It's too bad the French don't have a word for 'entrepreneur'.

George W. Bush

Ah well! I am their leader; I
really had to follow them!

Alexandre Auguste Ledru-Rollin

It will be sad if I either look up or
down after my death and don't see
my son fast asleep on the same
benches on which I have slept.

Lord Onslow

When the president does it, that
means that it is not illegal.

Richard Nixon

It is now a very good day to get out anything we want to bury.

Jo Moore on 11 September 2001

Nobody ever said it would be easy – and that was an understatement.

George Mitchell on the Northern Ireland peace talks

No woman in my time will be prime minister or chancellor or foreign secretary – not the top jobs.

Margaret Thatcher

All I know is that I'm not a Marxist.

Karl Marx

When we got into office, the thing that surprised me most was to find that things were just as bad as we'd been saying they were.

John F. Kennedy

I accept responsibility for everything that goes on in the MoD. But that does not mean that I'm to blame for everything.

Geoff Hoon

She is a loose cannon with
a sense of direction.

John Pienaar on Clare Short

It contains a misleading
impression, not a lie. It was being
economical with the truth.

Robert Armstrong

Pensioners were not born yesterday.

Steve Webb

MATERNITY WARD

I don't know what I would do without Whitelaw. Everyone should have a Willie.

Margaret Thatcher

Dear Chief Secretary,
I'm afraid there is no money.
Kind regards – and good luck!
Liam.

Liam Byrne in a letter to his successor

As God once said, and I think rightly...

Margaret Thatcher

I'll fight for what I believe in until I drop dead. And that's what keeps you alive.

Barbara Castle

This is an impressive crowd: the haves and the have-mores. Some people call you the elite. I call you my base.

George W. Bush

I don't know what reception I'm at, but for God's sake give me a gin and tonic.

Denis Thatcher

This is not a time for sound bites. We've left them at home. I feel the hand of history upon our shoulders.

Tony Blair

I'm worried about that young man. He's getting awfully bossy.

Margaret Thatcher on Tony Blair

I have often been accused of putting my foot in my mouth, but I have never put my hand in your pocket.

Spiro T. Agnew – later indicted for tax evasion

Honey, I forgot to duck.

Ronald Reagan to his wife, Nancy, after being shot

I experimented with marijuana a time or two. And I didn't like it, and I didn't inhale.

Bill Clinton

I suppose flattery hurts no one, that is, if he doesn't inhale.

Adlai Stevenson

There is no list and Syria isn't on it.

Jack Straw on the US description
of Syria as a rogue state

I don't mind how much my ministers
talk, as long as they do what I say.

Margaret Thatcher

The green belt is a Labour
achievement; and we intend
to build upon it.

John Prescott

I'm not going to have some reporters pawing through our papers. We are the president.

Hillary Clinton

My fellow Americans, I am pleased to tell you that I have signed legislation to outlaw Russia forever. We begin bombing in five minutes.

Ronald Reagan, asked to say something to test a microphone before an interview, presumably unaware he was being recorded

Outside of the killings, Washington has one of the lowest crime rates in the country.

Mayor Marion Barry

CONFERENCE CLASSICS

You were expecting me after all. On the way here I saw a cinema billboard which said: 'The Mummy Returns'.

Margaret Thatcher

So there you have it. The final proof. Labour's brand new shining modernist economic dream. But it wasn't Brown's. It was Balls'.

Michael Heseltine on reports that Gordon Brown's policies were developed by his young researcher Ed Balls

Now, many of us in the Labour Party are conservationists – and we all love the red squirrel. But there is one ginger rodent which we never want to see again in the Highlands – Danny Alexander.

Harriet Harman – at a Scottish Labour Party Conference

I've got a little list of
benefit offenders
who I'll soon be rooting out
And who never would be missed
They never would be missed
There's those who make
up bogus claims
In half a dozen names
And councillors who draw the dole
To run left-wing campaigns
They never would be missed
They never would be missed
Young ladies who get pregnant
just to jump the housing list
And dads who won't support
the kids of ladies they have... kissed
And I haven't even mentioned
all those sponging socialists
I've got them on my list
And there's none of them be missed
There's none of them be missed.

Peter Lilley

A one-legged army limping away from the storm they had created. Left! Left! Left! About turn! Right! Right! Right!

Michael Heseltine describing the Labour Party and then imagining new orders on the arrival of New Labour

'Can't get away to marry you today, my wife won't let me.'

James Callaghan singing a Marie Lloyd song at the party conference in an attempt to convince delegates that he hadn't set a date for the election

To those of you waiting with bated breath for that favourite media catchphrase, 'the U-turn', I have only this to say: 'You turn if you want to; the lady's not for turning.'

Margaret Thatcher

THE GREASY POLE

There are two kinds of chancellor. Those who fail and those who get out in time.

Gordon Brown

Office tends to confer a dreadful plausibility on even the most negligible of those who hold it.

Mark Lawson

Better to have him inside the tent pissing out, than outside pissing in.

Lyndon B. Johnson of J. Edgar Hoover

Ministers say one of two things in Cabinet. Some say, 'Look, Daddy. No hands.' Others say, 'Look, Daddy. Me too.'

Sarah Hogg

Healey's first law of politics: when you're in a hole, stop digging.

Denis Healey

Galbraith's law states that anyone who says he won't resign four times, will.

John Kenneth Galbraith

Being powerful is like being a lady. If you have to tell people you are, you aren't.

Margaret Thatcher

It is rather like sending your opening batsmen to the crease, only for them to find, as the first balls are being bowled, that their bats have been broken before the game by the team captain.

Geoffrey Howe on being undermined by Margaret Thatcher

Anyone can rat, but it takes a certain amount of ingenuity to re-rat.

Winston Churchill

There are only two ways of getting into the Cabinet. One way is to crawl up the staircase of preferment on your belly; the other way is to kick them in the teeth.

Aneurin Bevan

BROWN
NOSE
CHAMBERS

There's nothing so improves the mood of the Party as the imminent execution of a senior colleague.

Alan Clark

When you get to Number 10, you've climbed there on a little ladder called 'the status quo'. And when you're there the status quo looks very good.

Tony Benn

I never thought I would end up being the senator from New York. I never thought that the long-haired, bearded guy I married in law school would end up being president.

Hillary Clinton

TRIALS AND TRIBULATIONS

Normally when I'm asked on holiday and I say what I do, I say I'm a traffic warden. That makes me much more popular.

Steve Pound

It is difficult enough to go around doing what is right without going around trying to do good.

Lord Salisbury

The one thing I do not want to be called is First Lady. It sounds like a saddle horse.

Jacqueline Kennedy

Political image is like mixing cement. When it's wet, you can move it around and shape it, but at some point it hardens and there's almost nothing you can do to reshape it.

Walter Mondale

When I was a minister I always looked forward to the Cabinet meeting immensely because it was, apart from the summer holidays, the only period of real rest I got in what was a very heavy job.

Nigel Lawson

The vice-presidency isn't worth a pitcher of warm piss.

John Nance Garner

There are no true friends in politics.

Cicero

You want a friend in Washington? Get a dog.

Harry S. Truman

I spent several years in a North Vietnamese prison camp, in the dark... fed with scraps. Do you think I want to do that all over again as vice president of the United States?

John McCain

Are you depressed, unhappy, suicidal? Then think what it's like for me as a Conservative candidate?

John Kelly in his election address

An inconvenient house with three poor staircases.

Margot Asquith on life at Number 10

You're lucky to head a coalition government. I am a coalition government on my own.

John Major to the German Chancellor, Helmut Kohl

When I am asked by *Who's Who* what my interests are, I put DIY and gardening. Then I hope my wife won't read it.

Tony Newton

THE MEDIA

If Kinnock wins today, will the last person to leave Britain please turn out the lights.

Sun headline on Election Day 1992

I'm with you on the free press. It's the newspapers I can't stand.

Tom Stoppard

The difference between burlesque and the newspapers is that the former never pretended to be performing a public service by exposure.

I. F. Stone

Governments always tend to want, not really a free press, but a managed and well-conducted one.

Lord Radcliffe

If I blew my nose the *Daily Express* and the *Daily Mail* would say that I am trying to spread germ warfare.

Ken Livingstone

For a politician to complain about the press is like a ship's captain complaining about the sea.

Enoch Powell

When I go into the voting booth, do I vote for the person who is the best president? Or the slime bucket who will make my life as a cartoonist wonderful?

Mike Peters

The trouble with Twitter, the instantness of it – too many twits might make a twat.

David Cameron

Television has made dictatorships impossible, but democracy unbearable.

Shimon Peres

Never lose your temper with the press or the public is a major rule of political life.

Christabel Pankhurst

I read the newspapers avidly. It is my one form of continuous fiction.

Aneurin Bevan

Power without responsibility: the prerogative of the harlot throughout the ages.

Rudyard Kipling on press baron Lord Beaverbrook

Every sane and sensible and quiet thing we do is absolutely ignored by the press.

Bertrand Russell

Freedom of the press in Britain means freedom to print such of the proprietor's prejudices as the advertisers don't object to.

Hannen Swaffer

How is the world ruled and how do wars start? Diplomats tell lies to journalists and then believe what they read.

Karl Kraus

Nothing travels faster than the speed of light, with the possible exception of bad news, which obeys its own special laws.

Douglas Adams

If I want to knock a story off the front page, I just change my hairstyle.

Hillary Clinton

IT'LL END IN TEARS...

I have a young family and for the next few years I should like to devote more time to them.

Norman Fowler giving rise to the popular euphemistic resignation excuse of wanting to spend more time with the family

You actually see the moment when a man's political career leaves his body.

Jon Stewart on Gordon Brown's 'Bigotgate' moment

I thought Bigotgate was a shopping centre in Essex.

Frankie Boyle

My own view is that taping of conversations for historical purposes was a bad decision.

Richard Nixon

I have a lot of sympathy with him. I was too once a young bald leader of the Opposition.

Neil Kinnock on William Hague

I am Al Gore, and I used to be the next president of the United States of America.

Al Gore

You know the old saying: you win some, you lose some. And then there's that little-known third category.

Al Gore

Remember, they only name things after you when you're dead or really old.

Barbara Bush

Nothing is so abject and pathetic as a politician who has lost his job, save only a retired stud horse.

H. L. Mencken

I do believe that politicians would be far more ready to resign office if they did not feel that their doing so would give such infinite pleasure to their adversaries.

Lord Salisbury

All political lives, unless they are cut off in midstream at a happy juncture, end in failure, because that is the nature of politics and of human affairs.

Enoch Powell

Why should I accept the Order of the Garter from His Majesty when the people have just given me the Order of the Boot?

Winston Churchill

The penalty for success is to be bored by the people who used to snub you.

Nancy Astor

My chances of being PM are about as good as the chances of finding Elvis on Mars, or my being reincarnated as an olive.

Boris Johnson

I am humble enough to recognise that I have made mistakes, but politically astute enough to have forgotten what they are.

Michael Heseltine

There comes a time in every man's life when he must make way for an older man.

Reginald Maudling on being dropped from Margaret Thatcher's Shadow Cabinet and replaced by John Davies, who was one year older

Ever since I have been in the House I have been looked on as a might-be. Now I shall be a might-have-been.

Harold Nicolson on being dropped from Churchill's government

Has he resigned or has
he gone for a pee?

Margaret Thatcher on Michael Heseltine's
sudden departure from a Cabinet meeting

He has done the right thing, but
it is a pity the prime minister's
judgement led him to have to do it
twice in the space of one parliament.

William Hague on Peter Mandelson's
second resignation from the Cabinet

AND FINALLY…

History will be kind to me for I intend to write it.

Winston Churchill

Everyone in public life ought to be arrested at least once. It's an education.

Alan Clark

I have left orders to be awakened at any time in the case of a national emergency, even if I'm in a Cabinet meeting.

Ronald Reagan

We introduced the Community Charge. I still call it that. I like the Poles – I never had any intention of taxing them.

Margaret Thatcher

Responsibility without power, the prerogative of the eunuch throughout the ages.

Tom Stoppard on the House of Lords

We give the impression of being in office but not in power.

Norman Lamont

You campaign in poetry. You govern in prose.

Mario Cuomo

Politics has got so expensive that it takes a lot of money to even get beat with nowadays.

Will Rogers

Men enter local politics solely as a result of being unhappily married.

C. Northcote Parkinson

I share a bed with my wife – it does not make me a woman.

Tim Farron, Liberal Democrat President, on 'getting into bed' with the Conservatives

The House of Commons is the longest-running farce in the West End.

Cyril Smith

WEST END
WHOOPS, VICAR WHERE'S MY DISPATCH BOX!?

A politician is a person with whose politics you don't agree; if you agree with him he's a statesman.

David Lloyd George

You can't have a motion without a debate.

Hugh Dalton arguing with a nurse about whether he should have an enema

When in doubt what should be done, do nothing.

Lord Melbourne

Somewhere out in this audience may even be someone who will one day follow in my footsteps, and preside over the White House as the president's spouse. I wish him well!

Barbara Bush

There are two supreme pleasures in life. One is ideal, the other real. The ideal is when a man receives the seals of office from his Sovereign. The real pleasure comes when he hands them back.

Lord Rosebery

www.summersdale.com